Wolf Hill

Skydive Wedding

Roderick Hunt

Illustrated by Alex Brychta

Oxford University Press

OXFORD
UNIVERSITY PRESS

Great Clarendon Street, Oxford OX2 6DP

Oxford New York
Athens Auckland Bangkok Bogotá Buenos Aires Calcutta
Cape Town Chennai Dar es Salaam Delhi Florence Hong Kong Istanbul
Karachi Kuala Lumpur Madrid Melbourne Mexico City Mumbai
Nairobi Paris São Paulo Singapore Taipei Tokyo Toronto Warsaw

and associated companies in Berlin Ibadan

Oxford is a registered trade mark of Oxford University Press

© text Roderick Hunt 1999
© illustrations Alex Brychta
First Published 1999

ISBN 0 19 918744 4

Printed in Hong Kong

Chapter 1

Miss Teal was scared. Her arms felt numb. Her legs were like jelly. 'Why am I doing this?' she thought.

The door of the aircraft opened. She heard the roar of the engines. The wind slapped against her like giant hands. She closed her eyes.

She could feel John checking her harness. Then she heard his voice through the earpiece in her helmet.

'About thirty seconds to go,' she heard John say. 'Just relax.'

She felt John push her to the open door. 'I don't want to do this,' she shouted.

It was too late.

John shouted, 'Go! Go!' She felt a shove. Then they both jumped.

They fell like stones. The aircraft seemed to shoot upwards. Then the parachute opened. Miss Teal felt a jolt and suddenly she was floating.

There was no noise - just the rushing wind.

Miss Teal opened her eyes. Below her she could see fields and woods. They looked like patchwork. 'It's wonderful!' she said.

John's voice crackled in her ear piece. 'So are you,' he said. 'Will you marry me?'

Chapter 2

Mr Saffrey smiled at everyone. Then he locked his fingers and pushed his hands out. 'Click,' went his fingers.

'I wish he wouldn't do that,' said Kat.

'We want to say thank you to Miss Teal,' said Mr Saffrey. 'Do you know why?'

Lots of hands went up. 'Yes, Kirsty?' said Mr Saffrey.

'She did a parachute jump,' said a small girl in the front.

'That's right,' said Mr Saffrey. 'It was a sponsored jump. Miss Teal made £472 for the school computer fund.'

Everyone clapped. Some of the children cheered.

Mr Saffrey looked at Miss Teal. 'I have some more good news,' he said. Miss Teal blushed.

'Miss Teal is getting married,' went on Mr Saffrey. 'John asked her on the parachute jump. She said "Yes" before she reached the ground.'

Andy and Najma had a huge card for Miss Teal. It was a surprise from everyone in her class.

Miss Teal smiled. She had a surprise in store for her class.

Chapter 3

Miss Teal took her class to the airfield. They went by bus. John was there with the skydiving team.

'We're going to tell you about skydiving,' said John. 'Then, if the weather's OK, the team will show you a free fall.'

'Brilliant!' said Loz.

John showed everyone the plane. 'It's a Cessna,' he said. 'We jump out of this door.'

He let everyone sit inside it. 'I'd love to do a jump,' said Loz.

Andy wasn't so sure. The thought of jumping out of a plane scared him.

John showed them a parachute. 'We call it a canopy,' he said. 'It's very light. It opens when I pull this cord.'

'What happens if it doesn't work?' asked Michael Ward.

John smiled. 'That shouldn't happen,' he said. 'But if it does, we always have a second one to open.'

Chapter 4

The skydiving team had put up a tower. At the top they fixed a cable and a harness.

John clipped on the harness. Then he jumped off the tower. He came down slowly.

The cable was on a drum. It turned a big fan. The fan went round as John came down.

John said that everyone could have a go. He showed them how to land. 'It's quite safe,' he said. 'The fan acts as a brake.'

Andy was afraid when his turn came. John clipped a safety line to him. Then he helped him up the ladder.

At the top of the tower Andy felt giddy. It looked a long way down. He could see everyone looking up at him. 'Come on, Andy,' yelled Gizmo.

'It's no good,' said Andy. 'I can't do it.'

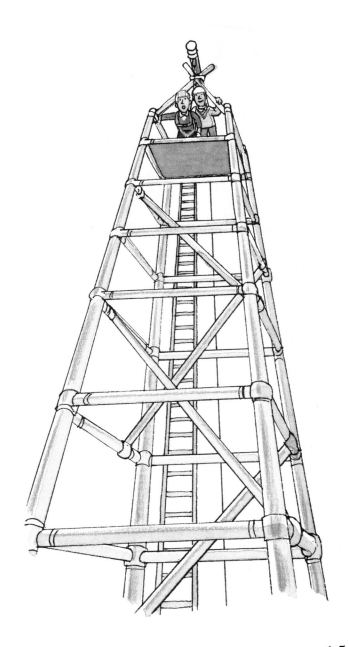

Chapter 5

John clipped the cable on to Andy's harness.

'I was scared the first time I did it,' he said. 'But it's easier to jump than climb back down the ladder. Just don't look down.'

'Go for it, Andy,' yelled Chris.

Andy felt his heart racing. His mouth was dry. He stood on the edge of the tower.

'Just step off,' said John. 'Keep your legs together. Bend your knees. Roll over as you land.'

Andy stepped off the tower.

It was the bravest thing he had ever done. The jump was over in a few seconds. He landed on the mat and rolled sideways.

'Wasn't it great?' said Loz. 'Imagine jumping out of an aeroplane. I'd love to.'

Andy didn't speak. His heart was beating too fast.

Chapter 6

It was time for the team to do the free fall. John looked up at the sky. The clouds were very dark.

Then it began to rain and a gusty wind blew.

'I'm sorry,' said John. 'We can't do a jump today. The wind is too strong. It wouldn't be safe.'

Everyone was disappointed.

Chris had a thought. 'Miss Teal,' he said. 'Why doesn't John skydive to your wedding?'

'It would be brilliant,' said Andy. 'He could land on the school field. We could see him skydiving after all.'

Miss Teal look at John and smiled. 'How about it?' she said.

'I think it's a great idea,' said John, 'and it's sure to be good weather for our wedding.'

John did skydive to the wedding. But things didn't go as Miss Teal planned.

Chapter 7

St Stephen's Church was near the school. That's where Miss Teal was getting married. Most of the children went to watch.

Everyone was excited. John was going to skydive on to the school field.

'Skydiving to the wedding was my idea,' said Chris.

'We know!' sighed Andy. 'You've *told* us that a million times.'

Some of the skydiving team were on the field. They had put down a big white cross. That was where John was going to land.

Loz was first to see something.
'There it is,' she called. Everyone
gazed at the sky. There was a plane
very high up. It was quite a long way
off.

All eyes watched the plane.
Suddenly there were two trails of
smoke in the sky.

It was John and his best man. They were free falling. They had smoke guns strapped to their legs.

One skydiver's parachute opened. The other skydiver went on falling. 'That's John,' someone said. 'I hope he's not in trouble.'

Chapter 8

John seemed to fall a long way. At last his canopy opened. Everyone sighed. 'Phew!' said Andy. 'That's why skydiving scares me.'

John began to circle quite fast. 'He's using his emergency parachute,' said a man. 'He's coming down too quickly.'

Everyone could see John clearly. He seemed to skim over the school roof. Then he dropped down on to the field.

He hit the ground hard. He rolled over and lay still for a second. Then he got up. Seconds later, John's best man landed lightly beside him.

Everyone cheered, but something was wrong. John tried to walk, but his leg gave way. He fell back on the grass.

'He's hurt his leg,' said Najma. 'I hope he's all right. I hope he can get to the wedding.'

John was not all right. He had twisted his ankle badly. 'Ouch!' he said. 'I don't think I can walk.'

Mr Saffrey looked at John's ankle. 'It's very swollen,' he said. 'Oh dear! You'll have to borrow the school wheelchair.'

'I'll never live this down,' said John.

Chapter 9

Something else went wrong.
Everyone was waiting. But Miss Teal
was late. She was very late.

The children waited outside the
church. Miss Teal's class stood on
each side of the church path. 'I wish
she'd come,' said Chris. I'm tired of
this.'

'Something's happened,' said John. 'She should have been here half an hour ago.'

'It could be the traffic,' said his best man. 'There is a huge traffic jam in town. We saw it from the air.'

A mobile phone rang. The best man answered it. He pulled a face. 'Oh no!' he said. 'Right! I'll tell John.'

It was bad news. The whole town was at a standstill. Miss Teal was stuck in the traffic. The wedding car was on West Bridge.

Mr Saffrey spoke to the children. 'I'm afraid Miss Teal won't be here for ages. The town is gridlocked.'

Everyone felt sorry for Miss Teal. Her wedding wasn't going as she expected.

'What a shame,' said Loz.

Then Arjo had a brilliant idea. It was an idea that saved Miss Teal's wedding.

Chapter 10

Arjo told Kat what his idea was. 'It's a great idea, Arjo,' said Kat. 'Tell Mr Saffrey.'

Arjo tugged Mr Saffrey's sleeve. 'What is it, Arjo?' said Mr Saffrey.

'Use the canal,' said Arjo.

Mr Saffrey didn't catch what Arjo was saying. 'What do you mean, Arjo?' he said.

'Miss Teal could come by boat,' said Arjo. 'She could come along the canal.'

'You're a genius, Arjo,' said Mr Saffrey. 'It's not far from West Bridge along the canal. We could drive Miss Teal up the lane from the allotments. But how do we get hold of a boat?'

'My uncle's got one,' said Gizmo. 'He'll be down at the canal now.'

'Right,' said Mr Saffrey. 'Let's go. We'll take the school minibus.' He looked at Gizmo. 'You and Arjo can both come,' he said. 'You can talk to your uncle. I just hope he agrees to this.'

Kat looked at Loz, Andy, Chris and Najma. 'May we all come?' she asked.

'Oh, all right,' said Mr Saffrey, 'but I don't know what Miss Teal will say.'

Chapter 11

Gizmo's uncle was down by the canal. He was working on his boat. He looked surprised when Gizmo turned up with Mr Saffrey.

'It's an emergency,' said Mr Saffrey. He told Gizmo's uncle about Miss Teal. 'She's stuck on West Bridge. It will take ages to get to the church by road.'

'Right,' said Gizmo's uncle. 'We'll go and get her by boat. We can be there in five minutes.' He started up the motor.

'Hang on,' said Chris. 'This boat doesn't look too clean. If Miss Teal has a white dress it could get dirty.'

Mr Saffrey ran to the minibus. He came back with a huge roll of paper.

'We'll cover the floor with clean paper,' he said. 'The minibus is full of art stuff. It's lucky I forgot to take it out.'

The boat was quite small. There wasn't room for everyone. 'Arjo can come,' said Mr Saffrey. 'The rest of you wait by the minibus.'

Najma looked in the minibus. 'There's paint, paper, Blu-tak, scissors,' she said. 'I've got an idea, but we'll have to be quick. We've only got a few minutes.'

Chapter 12

Miss Teal's car wasn't on West Bridge. The traffic had moved a little. The car was a few metres the other side.

Mr Saffrey sprinted up to it. He tapped on the window. 'We've come to rescue you,' he said. 'We can get you to the church in ten minutes.'

Miss Teal was in the car with her father. They got out and walked to the canal. Miss Teal was wearing a beautiful white dress. 'How will I get on to that little boat in this?' she said.

Miss Teal's father laughed. 'Mr Saffrey and I will carry you,' he said. 'Come on!'

Chapter 13

The minibus looked different. Andy and Loz had made paper flowers. They had stuck them over the back door. The others had made two banners. They had put one on each side.

The banners said, '*To Miss Teal. Good Luck from Wolf Hill School.*'

They had just finished in time. The boat pulled up as Loz stuck on the last paper flower.

Mr Saffrey and Miss Teal's father carried her to the allotment. Miss Teal laughed when she saw the minibus.

'It looks great!' she said. 'Thank you for making it look so special. Who wants a big white wedding car? This is much better.'

Miss Teal looked at Arjo. 'Thank you, Arjo. It was your idea to use the canal.' Then she gave Arjo a kiss.

Arjo pretended to faint. He fell backwards into a bush.

'Come on,' said Mr Saffrey. 'Let's get you to the church.' He started the minibus. 'By the way, there's something we haven't told you. It's about John.'

Chapter 14

Miss Teal came out of the church with John. His best man pushed the wheelchair.

Everyone cheered as they walked down the path.

'She's not Miss Teal any longer,' said Andy. 'By the way, what is her name now?'

'I think she's Mrs Gray,' said Loz.

A lady was taking photographs. Miss Teal wanted a picture by the school minibus.

There was one more surprise. A helicopter flew overhead. It came lower and lower.

'Look,' said Arjo. 'It's landing on the school field.'

John grinned at Miss Teal. 'You've always wanted to fly in a helicopter,' he said. 'Now is your chance.'

'I'll get back in the minibus,' said Miss Teal. 'Mr Saffrey can drive us to the school field.'

'There's no need,' said Mr Saffrey. 'The wedding car is here at last. You ought to go in that.'

Chapter 15

Everyone went to the school field. The helicopter was at the far end.

The wedding car drove across the playground. As it got to the field, it slowed down.

Miss Teal wound the window down and threw her bouquet. It sailed towards Chris. He held out his hands and caught it. Then he went bright red.

Everyone laughed.

'See you next term, Miss Teal,' called Najma. 'Will you come by helicopter?'

'Or skydive to school?' said Loz.

'You must be joking,' said Mrs Gray.